# Praise for
# *Limbolandia*

*Limbolandia* arrives to remind us that we continue to cross, be it along the US/Mexican border, ordering in a Frankfurt, Germany restaurant, during a desert hallucinated crucifixion, on a bus in London, England, in a morgue, or from the longing for another. It is in this perpetual passage that Esteban Rodríguez writes to remember that regardless of exclusion, inclusion, or absence, there is a transformation in our humanity through that movement. The poet conjures startling imagery and tenderness as "flower petals: forget-me-nots, orchids, rhododendrons" are pulled from "the wound" and manage to spill "dead butterflies" from the mouths of the dead "like communion wafers." He applies the surreal to guide us toward understanding our existence, yet also invites us into open love letters that become sites to re-assert longing and "move with gestures our tongues won't feel the need to interpret." Rodríguez is a poet with a coiled verse, simultaneously at the precipice of strike and stillness, allowing language to absorb the speed of the world and uncover moments for "praising... the privileged shadows that don't let themselves be erased" as we await our next crossing.

—Anthony Cody

The analytical cool of these poems defies any easy label you want to put on them. That's part of the pleasure in reading them: if the poet explores social identity, he's also impatient with the restrictive nature of that category. If he ventures into the visionary, it's never the hokey, apocalyptic kind which is almost a period style nowadays. If he's intent on precise description— "the trailer park elders" who "lumber /onto lawn chairs, jam their hands inside//their mouths, pry their dentures out, and dip/the rotted implants into buckets and spittoons,/as though attempting to deep-fry the false enamel,//saturate old inflections into a semblance/of speech they can finally chew…" —you can see that he does a lot more than give a printout. The fidelity of image to those dentures is bent, subtly strange, but without the strain of the surreal. And as the perceptions modulate and unfold, you can see how the lines and syntax reinforce each other. He writes real lines, not slapdash expressionist junk. Most importantly, passion in these poems isn't only feeling things and then declaiming, *Oh! Look at me feeling them!* For this poet, writing poems is a mode of serious inquiry—intellectual, spiritual, emotional, and deeply ironic. And such seriousness and strangeness inform every line of this work.

—Tom Sleigh

# LIMBOLANDIA

FLOWERSONG
PRESS

Poems by

## Esteban Rodríguez

FLOWERSONG
PRESS

FlowerSong Press
Copyright © 2023 by Esteban Rodríguez
ISBN: 978-1-953447-37-1
Library of Congress Control Number: 2023932263

Published by FlowerSong Press
in the United States of America.
www.flowersongpress.com

Cover Image by Iris Perez
Set in Adobe Garamond Pro

NOTICE: SCHOOLS AND BUSINESSES
FlowerSong Press offers copies of this book at quantity discount with bulk
purchase for educational, business, or sales promotional use. For information,
please email the Publisher at info@flowersongpress.com.

# CONTENTS

**A Crossing**

## Limbolandia

## The Love Letters of José _____

# LIMBOLANDIA

# A Crossing

# I

So I said I am José, and the wind
turned its back, left me a scene I knew

I wouldn't understand: buzzards, carcass,
a cactus casting shade with the burden

of metaphor. And because my body, half
clothed and unbalanced, was wounded

with days of trekking, I moved closer,
took in the details of this feast,

of the way beaks tore through flesh, bone,
how they made the hide an easy simile,

how this language scrawled across the ground
was one my tongue would never own,

but which I didn't care to own, so long
as I could walk though this heap,

so long as I believed that on the other side
of scenes like these, there'd be a new home.

## II

I nudge him, speak the name
he gave us with the conviction

of prayer, but he doesn't move.
And as the sun yawns across

the horizon, and we eat the last
of our food, we accept that Lalo

will not be coming with us,
that we must close his eyelids,

mumble something genuine,
meaningful, and be glad, as much

as we don't want to, that this isn't us,
or that when we woke up in the morning

we weren't forced onto the back
of a truck, or made to call our families

back home, demand they make
a payment we knew they couldn't afford.

No, we merely put our backpacks on,
and after saying the names of our daughters,

sons, take a deep breath and move deeper
into the desert, guilty, as we were

the day before, that we could put
one foot in front of the next.

# III

Before sunset, God appears to me
as a shadow. But in the morning

when the group I entered the desert with
is nowhere to be found, God is a small boy,

shirtless, barefoot, mouth caked with sweat
and saliva. Without saying a word, he asks me

to follow, and because I am starving,
because water and the idea of water

have become folklore, I move behind Him,
weave through rock after cactus after rock,

until, what feels like days later, God and I
arrive at a cross. And of course, there are nails

below it, and I know the moment God
reaches for them I will have to hoist Him up,

and with strength I didn't know I possessed,
will have to tell God goodbye, then hammer

every nail through his flesh.

# Frankfurt

At the Adolf Wagner, you ask
for blood sausage, and the server,
in English his tone clearly has contempt
for, asks if you're sure, if you know
what you're ordering, if, by any chance,
you've ever had this before.
And of course, to save face,
you say yes, yes you have,
and the server—skeptical of your body
language, response—nods, walks away.
You see him laugh at a table nearby,
imagine he's cracking jokes
at your expense, and you can't help
but think of your father, how
at restaurants back in Texas,
he tenses up, says, when the server
asks for drinks, *Tea, Sweet tea please*,
but with Spanish still heavy on his lips,
still fatigued with uncertainty, diaspora,
with thinking that once he crossed over,
his tongue would have a newfound
confidence, and he'd speak like you
speak now, sharp with every consonant,
tender with every vowel.

# IV

From afar, they appear to be floating,
apparitions meant to wander the heat

and uncertainty. And when close enough,
I recognize them for the group I entered

the desert with, only they have pieces
of their bodies missing: arm, foot, eyes

that appear to be ripped from their skulls.
And some have their guts hanging out.

And others carry their tongues in their hands—
a symbol I ignore because when the group

surrounds me, when, without saying a word,
they let me know they're glad they found me,

I understand the symbol doesn't matter,
that I've crossed a threshold where I am

no longer hungry, thirsty, and where
this journey, regardless of the reasons

I began it, no longer feels like a burden.

# V

When the river appears,
I move toward it, take off

the crusted remnants of my boots,
button-down, corduroys.

And when I arrive at the river,
it's everything I expected,

a chance to cleanse the dirt
and debris on every open wound,

every scabbed crevice, until
the river, like any promise,

can no longer hold its end
of the bargain, and I am left

in a ditch, cold, naked, unsure
what night will bring when

the sun deserts the horizon,
and when I must trek back

to my clothes, wonder if putting
them back on will provide

a sense of safety, comfort.

# VI

For days darkness.
Then we're ushered out,

and the truck takes off,
stains the horizon as a small

black dot, while we,
still laying our shadows

on the ground, are told
that when we begin to walk,

we must keep our heads
down, our mouths shut,

must traverse the terrain
as if we were walking

on sacred ground,
or as if there were spirits

lingering about, and commotion—
our commotion—would truly

wake them up. And so, for days
we stay silent, let only sweat

escape the most restless parts
of our skin, even at night,

when creatures in the distance
begin to howl, and we must wipe

our anonymity from our lips,
must listen to the sound of teeth

breaking a being's will, flesh, bone.

# VII

Then I see a hand rise from the ground,
and out comes God, bloody, dusty,

still the boy He was when I nailed Him
to the cross, only this time He is smiling,

as if He knew this would happen,
that I would do what I thought was my job.

Before I can ask if it was a test,
or to what extent I passed, a ball appears

at His feet, and He kicks it toward me,
expecting that I return the pass, so that,

I assume, after an afternoon of doing this,
I will have no longer thought about what is

and isn't real, if God is truly in front of me,
or if the circumstances that brought me here

were indeed beyond my control. No,
I would merely focus on the ball, certain,

of this at least, that I can make something
come to life on this desert ground.

# London

November, and London is just
as you expected. And on the bus
back to the center of the city,
you hear the woman in front of you
speaking Spanish, not the one
of Spain, but of your grandparents,
mother, father, of a Mexico you weren't
born in, but which you'd visit, spend
weekends getting haircuts, fruit, vegetables,
or visiting pharmacies for ailments
your mother hadn't been diagnosed with,
but which she suspected, no, which she knew.

You wonder how the woman
in front of you arrived here, if she,
as a professor claimed in college,
was part of a wave that was skipping
the United States, headed to England,
Europe, because work was not an empty
promise, but a chance to clock out
for the day, ride the bus, and on the way
back home—in view of Big Ben, the Shard—
phone a relative or friend, and not care
who listened to her call.

## Punta Cana

If you were someone else,
you'd think it was fate,
that on your way to the dining hall,
eager to return to your room
with two, maybe even three plates,
you were meant to be called to,
that it was some higher plan that you
were stopped, and with the walkway
packed, and nowhere to move,
you had to stay, listen to one of three
men at the booth, to how he said
*My friend, my friend* in such confident
English, raised the necklace
in his hand like a serpent,
and told you you could have this
for twenty dollars. If you
were someone else, you would have
turned him down quickly, smiled
and walked away, and not felt guilty,
thought about what it means
to be born in a different country,
that if your mother and father
had stayed in Mexico, your life would
have been different, and perhaps you,
like this man, would be selling necklaces
to tourists, bargaining, bargaining,
until you found a price you could live with.

## VIII

At first, we believe it's a hat,
or perhaps a glove, or the remnants

of a rag that someone tossed
on the ground, no longer worried

about the sweat on their brow,
or the sweat that pooled in their eyelids,

gave every mirage a mirage.
But when the group and I come close

to it, I see it's none of this at all,
but instead
                        a heart,
                                    yes
        a heart,


                        small,
        dark,
                        shriveled


                                    like a deflated
ball, and in this moment, the most

beautiful thing I had seen,
because perhaps, even though it had

clearly been ripped out, it wasn't
displayed as a warning or lesson,

but a symbol of hope, a beacon
that urged me to pick it up,

and once pressed against my ear,
to wait, listen.

# IX

*A circus*, they said. *We're a circus.*
And I question why the ringmaster

doesn't use the past tense, why he hasn't
seen himself for what he is: a ragged,

makeup-smeared man who believes
the people behind him are what they claim

to be: juggler, sword-swallower,
a large, bearded lady. And though

they want to show me, convince
our group that they are still entertaining,

we say no, and instead offer them
what's left of our food and water,

to which the ringmaster, standing
slowly, says no, no, that they no longer

need it, that the desert has cured them
of their thirst, hunger, and we, like them,

will soon need nothing for bodies,
that all we'll have to do—forever, forever—

is wake up each morning, wander.

Limbolandia

## Motel 6, Texas

You awake to a family not your own.
Your new mother, braless in a black
tank top, sits smoking by the windowsill.

Your sister, slurping on a snow cone,
stands next to an uncle whose mustache alone
suggests he kisses family members,

lips and all. He's out cold. The vent
above the couch, gagging on its rust,
ruffles his shiny toupee, and as you study

his brown corduroys, the plaid button-down,
the white snakeskins adorned with metallic
flames, you look down, see that you too

are wearing the same. But the yellow lei
around your neck is new, overly festive,
and though you want to see an island

scrunched between the window frame—
palm trees, waves, overweight tourists
melting on the shore—there's only desert,

complete with a cactus on each end,
and a band of tumbleweeds in mid-migration,
wary of anything that might interrupt

their symbolism. The room, of course,
has its own: chipped wood panels,
leaky pipe stains, floral wallpaper edged

with spider nests well past their weekly stays.

And there's a towel acting as a curtain
slung beside a milk carton acting

as an ashtray, which your mother
nearly topples as she taps her cigarette,
turns away, expecting you, it seems,

to keep watch over something that hasn't
happened yet, and that won't, not today,

not while the dust devils in the distance
struggle to keep form, too fatigued

to carve their own space.

# Fossors

Though dusk got bored of us,
sought sympathy from softer soil,
the council of crows, perched on power lines

and fence posts, continued their cawing,
announcing that the war was over,
that death, like a maze, did indeed

have an end. And what exact conflict
were they cawing of, what tragedies
and collateral damage had they witnessed,

remained uncertain, their crow politics
a distraction for the plots we were
commissioned—or was it indentured?—

to dig. We made crosses of tree bark,
feeling religious when the splinters raked us,
carved stigmatas on our wrists. We chiseled

inscriptions with our fingernails, invented
names and dates, chronicled family histories
we started to believe in, going back far enough

to add folklore, violence, fame. And when we
reached a point meant for gods and goddesses—
each ripe with jealousy—we rehearsed

our alibis instead, convincing ourselves
that you had always been my caretaker,
and that I, worn from hallowing the earth,

a drifter who no longer remembered
his name.

# Fair

All afternoon, you wander the park,
watch the clowns who've been confined
to crutches and casts drag bundles

of deflated balloons. For a moment,
as the helium seeps out, you imagine blood
flowing from the necks of every pony,

elephant, giraffe, each forming a trail
of puddles your bare feet will soon feel.
Summer renders you shoeless, offers

no explanations, just funnel cakes sugared
with spider webs, turkey legs mauled
by crows complementing the canopy

of clouds crosshatched with overcast,
cotton candy the flavor of communion
wafers, teddy bears stuffed with dead

honeybees—their plush blackened
from the grease dripping off the hands
of carnies who scoff every time you win,

break the pyramids of vases with softballs
made of small skulls. And why skulls?
Are they real? Whose faces had to be

melted, peeled? You should but don't care,
and don't need to when the stilt walkers
juggle machetes in circles, or when ring

after ring of flames erupt from their mouths,

flash against a backdrop of dusk worthy
of motivational posters, and refocus

your attention to the roller coasters
jutting out like the fossilized spines
of creatures found in folktales; the metal

humps lost to the spokes of fireworks
sprouting across the deep-fried darkness,

one by one by one by one.

# La Isla

There was sand everywhere. Of course,
the island would have it no other way,
and the placeboed destiny you prescribed

yourself wouldn't either. How else
did the local children—whose faces
had been scalded, erased—bury you,

clump a ring of sand around your throat,
place a plastic bucket on your head,
and insist, in their blistered voices,

that this was the best way to enjoy paradise?
You were buried there for years.
The gulls grew tired of your flesh,

lost their appetite on your scabbed lips,
and the crabs, giants given your point of view,
made it their duty to keep you awake,

clipping an eyelash every time an eyelid
gave meaning to gravity, every time
your head sunk back in on your vertebrae.

Tourists came and went, squatted, smiled,
snapped photo after photo, graffitied
what was left of your face, and at night

ran stark naked across you, letting
the moonlight shampoo their foreign
and fetal bodies. You should have been

envious—you were the one without arms
or legs. You should have shimmied out,
joined them, let the cold cold water seep

into every gap of your sand-filled frame,
or with what remained of your teeth,
you should have marked an SOS when the gulls

and crabs weren't looking, been daring,
mutinous, embodied an adjective that implied
you weren't merely watching as the kites—

scuttling the horizon—lost their sense
of weightlessness, and waited, so patiently,
for the wind to inter them beneath the waves.

# Roundabout

As if the pasture were made for fugitives,
you walk into it, come upon a herd
of wooden horses, hand-carved, hand-

painted, mounted onto springs,
and bobbing out of the silhouettes
they've been placed in, stallionesque,

you think, because you can't find a modifier
that's better suited, and don't want one,
not after you touch their splintered faces,

run your hand along their hoofless legs,
then tap your nails on every inch of their chipped
and sun-warped manes, until you settle

on the saddles worn with years of shoe-marks
left by the swinging feet of children.
A gallop echoes behind you. You think

you smell cotton candy. You think
you hear music playing, the crescendo
of clarinets and accordions, followed

by instruments with more than one name.
And as you push through the fog's fetal web,
unweave the haziness that leaves

the time of day open for interpretation,
you find a shoveled pit and a pile
of porcelain dolls stacked into a poorly

shaped pyramid, the symbolism which is,
even for you, overly sentimental, obvious
to the point that when you begin tossing in

the dolls, flinging them from their limbless
sockets, the hint of nostalgia that renders
your body gooseflesh feels diluted,

heavy-handed, too eager to frame objects
within the context of a larger picture,
and to get you to use outdated idioms

that make you believe a larger picture
existed in the first place, that everything
requires a connection, or at best deserves

the illusion that some part of it
is predestined, which is why you drop
the dolls and follow the glow growing brighter

in your periphery, certain the figures
shifting behind it are searching
for someone to share their burden.

# Pilgrims

At the bus stop, women in white dresses
shake milk jugs full of holy water,
ready to bless a city whose street names

are numbers, and whose buildings,
old and deserted, resemble miles
of coral, oddly shaped and porous,

weathered of their color, and guarded
by sweat-soaked soldiers wearing baggy
uniforms. There are goats tethered to lampposts.

There are Christmas lights piled by trash bins,
boxes of old snow that won't melt.
Dogs piss in potholes, and droves

of barefoot children walk around dragging
dead pets. The vendors sell either watches
or insurance, commodities that bare

no distinction, and as you scan the market—
the tables filled with jars of ashes
from old wars, the wheelchaired fortune tellers

adorned with ferrets and pearls—a man
with a tin foil hat escorts you to a chair,
where you sit watching him twirl a piece

of cardboard, unsure if his performance
counts as a souvenir.

# Cathedral

Every night you wander
a different city, and every dawn,
as the sun fevers the bomb-

speckled streets and sidewalks,
you remember, quite suddenly,
the tattered and graffitied signage,

the mounds of old trash and ribcages,
and the cathedral behind the labyrinth
of cardboard houses; how strange it feels

to cross yourself when you enter,
and yet how calm you are when the altar
begins burning, when the fire redefines

the candle stands, tabernacle, the frescoes
with figures dividing the earth into hell
and heaven. You move down the aisle,

survey the spotty congregation,
question why a flock still remains.
And though you think about dropping

to your knees, chanting your own form
of atonement, you ascend the altar,
untouched by the flames, and unwilling

to let anything hinder you from ad-libbing
a sermon, or from citing dates and mandates
that feel archaic on your tongue,

but familiar enough to remind you
that as ash rains down, casts a crown
on your head, you'll return tomorrow

evening, ready to carry out
your rites again.

# Ward

Above you, the fluorescent lights flicker,
buzz, beckon the orbs of homeless gnats
to sacrifice their lives for a common cause,

yet refuse to accept a description that will
complement the body bag you unzip
yourself from, or that will capture the urgency

with which you sit up, take your blindfold off,
and begin regurgitating the dead butterflies
lodged in your mouth. Like communion wafers,

you cup them in your palms, ponder their origins,
their migration from a distant country to the pale
surface of your tongue, and sensing that the ritual

you've become the center of isn't yet done—
the butterflies convulsing, as though something
inside wants out—you toss them on the ground,

thinking that as they dissolve into black confetti,
the act of putting distance between an object
and your body will lessen the uncertainty you feel.

Still, you can't help but adjust your gown,
but set your feet on the tiles and follow the small,
misshapen shadows that scuttle the walls,

but listen as the laughter, echoing at the end
of each hall, leads you to a door with light
pulsing from the bottom—the glow throbbing

with such excessiveness, that as you walk in
and see a full-length mirror in the middle
of the room, you know the glass won't reflect

the figure you thought you once knew.

## Scarecrows

Forty days in, and that phase
between late winter and consciousness
places you in an empty field.

You blink once, see a sea
of decommissioned scarecrows,
their pumpkin faces rotted, peeled.

You blink twice, and the shudder
renders them on fire, the flames
turning blue, brighter, their arms

unraveling, extending wider, wider;
minor crucifixions, you think,
for a ritual you can't name

nor remember, or for that vague
feeling that mimics the manner
in which you move between them,

unfazed at how slowly—hay figure
after figure—they twist their torsos,
keep their gaze on you, and begin

chanting in a language that feels
as if it had hung for decades
on a tree branch, sun-scorched

and deciduous, and all the more bitter
in your mouth when you, still weaving
aimlessly amongst them, start to hum

what you assume is the verse and chorus,
raising your pitch until the bruised orb
of dusk yawns above the flames,

and you're compelled to rest
your head against a scarecrow's
ash-coated leg, patiently decomposing,

like a sinned body after
it's been burned at the stake.

## Sideshow

We stumble upon a pair of cages,
and like children, feel the need
to touch them, to wonder why

their frames are gnawed on, caved in,
sun-warped and dented, angled
in every adjective we have yet to think of,

since our minds, caught between sleep
and delirium, can't recall the reasons
we've trudged miles of fetal darkness

to arrive here. Maybe they're built for us,
you say, maybe our masters are waiting,
have already concocted punishments

for passing curfew. But when no one comes up
to claim us, when we find ourselves free
of barcodes or markings, we accept our role

as spectators, lend our shadows to a line
of half-naked men, perched like gargoyles
on a pyramid of milk crates, displaying

the myriad of faces tattooed to their faces;
to a bearded baroness, decked in jawbones
and snake skin, eating bucket after bucket

of fish heads; to the androgynous Siamese twins
wearing latex, sipping their own whispers
from a chalice. And though I don't hear them

ask us to come closer like you do, don't listen
to what short-lived language they will
feed us, I feel their scripted odes

on my shoulders, the way the blindfolded
woman, hanging from some medieval
contraption, can feel the hook on hers;

her skeleton of a body swaying in such sharp
and strange angles that we think the wind
is trying to seduce us. And even if

the breeze stroking our flesh feels familiar,
we know there's more to see deeper
down the strip: children in buffalo heads,

bikinied women with legs hanging
from their hips, cyclopes with topknots,
men with elephantiasis, clowns juggling

pickled punks and jars of testicles shaped
like jellyfish, and a circle of crosshatched figures
dancing just beyond the tents, chanting

around a bonfire, waiting for us to undress,
to toss our new voices into that swollen pit.

# Ciudad

In the old city, the sidewalks bear
the prologue of December's burden:
sludge and snow lay clumped

against upturned garbage bins,
flaccid sandbags, cathedrals of rotting
cardboard, abandoned shopping carts

filled with suitcases and mattresses.
You pass a pair of mannequins
dressed in trench coats and gas masks.

You pass another, then another,
then notice that the farther you lumber
around every street corner—conceding

to nightfall's subtle shift in reason,
perception—the more the mannequins
clutter into groups, follow your trail,

stare without truly staring as you begin
searching for something you think
you once hid in the city: a trinket,

a postcard coded with doodles
and hieroglyphics, a whisper you stuffed
in a shoebox, expecting those soft syllables

to grow into a narrative, or a fable,
or a story within a story that draws
the protagonist to the middle of an alley,

where he—part-citizen, part-part-time
investigator—stumbles upon a chalk outline,
and, aware of the obstacles and adversaries

behind him, lies down and contorts his limbs
to fit within the lines of that drawing,
wondering if the moon, peeking above

the polluted buildings, will find his body
as sufficient evidence.

# The Love Letters of José _____

**Dear** _____,

After myths   fables   after legends still
preserved in rumored tableaux   our graves begin
to move away from us   We survey
the world's velvet lawns   the overgrown
foliage kneeling on the side of every road
reposing for autumn's uncommitted sun
No one feature is extraordinary   you say
and yet   your laugh   in profile   echoes
through memory's lonely chambers
I call out   and the staircase you descend
refuses to accept my voice

# Dear _____,

When the rain stopped   you ventured forth
descended the polished slopes   moving
with a logic the air couldn't attest to
until   days later   you came upon a cabin
approached its sunken porch
and the pair of porcelain dolls resting
just below it   The one nearest
you professed   assumed my appearance
and though you felt the need to touch it
run your fingers along my weathered skin
the wind stirred toward a different ending
At dusk   the crows caw on the rooftop
and our bodies   fractured   sexless
lie on the sodden ground

# Dear _____,

Beneath the chandelier   we sway unimpeded
my hand on your waist   yours on my gilded
epaulette   Our legs blur   shift in circles across
the dance floor   and because language cannot
capture the reasons behind each step   we don't
question the uniform   the dress   how silent
the crowd becomes when we stop   stare
at the ways in which their regal outlines begin
to blend   The orchestra intermits   The room grows
smaller   Tonight   love   the harpist will forget
her notes   and our limbs   tangled   distorted
will move with gestures our tongues won't feel
the need to interpret

# Postcard

In Texas   I left you on a swing set   watching
the sun haul itself toward that corner of the earth
you confessed you saw yourself dead in   buried
beneath the shadows of tumbleweeds   cactuses
I pushed you closer toward the sky's hemorrhage
while you   with those complacent strands of hair
masked to your mouth   described how you wanted
your chest tattooed in calaveras   as though I'd be the one
to lean on your jaundiced body   color in the skulls
till I covered your ribs   breasts   and clavicles
and placed bouquets of roses where your ears once were
The more you spoke of their designs   how their foreheads
should have a keyhole or cross   the more I remembered
in some state up north   late December   snow unfurling
its homeless breath across the city's streets
and rooftops   you left me untangling a labyrinth
of blankets and bedsheets   searching for your whispers
beneath the pillows   your mumbles amongst the folds
And when I found your voice curled along my navel
trembling   concerned   I scooped it in my palm
separated the inflections from the words
and watched as it began to flutter like an injured bird
the squeals so harsh   that I placed it in a shoebox
left it on the floor   and waited   with each step back
I took   for the slurs to resemble the echo of music
dying in the distance

# Dear _____,

Eyes lifted to the ceiling   we commence
a song   Call it pride   desire   Call it a gesture
where hands are raised toward the windows
the want to leave foggy palm prints on the stained
glass   Call it a moment in which people bow
their heads   while we   poised with a look
we seldom inhabit   stare at one another
from across the room   We'll always be novice
at this   you mouth again   and the choir
on cue   leads us through another verse
Incense clouds the aisles   Women adjust
their jewelry   Echoes settle on the paintings
and the sunlight at the door kneels
to our shadows

# Dear _____,

Morning   and the stammering streaks
of darkness recede from the windowpane
All night   we've lied awake   learned
the rhythm of a broken faucet   redrawn
the maps of old ceiling stains   Our bodies
fluent in hotel sheets   skipped formalities
and sunk   half-dressed and fevered   into
the weak and burdened springs   You rose
without your shadow   ambled toward the window
where you waited for the glass to render
your features into focus   in much the way
that I sat up   stared at the phone beside me
unsure how long it'd be before it rang

**Dear _____,**

That winter   we composed vignettes about the sea
an overcast coast filled with sunken headstones
a beach with a horde of ships capsized evenly
along the sand   We could not tell what sentiment
the clouds objected to   but when a convent began
to form around a gallows   each cloaked figure
holding a censer   humming a psalm   we ambled
toward the water   rinsed our foggy hands
In those moments   the tide had no choice
but to love us back   and though we ought to have
opened the trunks the sea dragged forth for us
we merely sat   watched the waves attempt
to kiss our cold and callused feet

**Dear _____,**

The furniture has been removed
Fashions have changed   The imperfect light
swells with carvings of broken crosses
cherubs' heads   We page through Hebrew verses
antiquated and half-effaced   wrought with fingers
that have feigned intimacy with generations
of coffin dust   All these relics hush the night's
heavy beds   Shut the door   old friend   let us
rinse our effigies in the puddles of moonlight
our ghosts will soon forget how to confess to

# Dear _____,

Tonight   even the moon remains an expatriate
and the tableful of people we are seated with
decent   curious   speak about a storm   an ocean
a shore bearing a constellation of charred remains
and half-buried remnants   Their voices encourage
reason   yet your stare into the caffeinated distance
invites December into the subplot of this narrative
where you   cold and fully dressed   walk along
the beach   weave through the ancient wreckage
and follow a trail of footsteps frozen in the sand
After the stars have scuttled to their corners
the breeze will tug our scarfs   lead us past
the shattered wings   the heap of delicate engines

# Postcard

Beneath bundles of rubberband-bound letters
origami fortune tellers   and undated Polaroids
yellowed at the edges   I pulled fragments
of your voice from a shoebox   shook out
the sighs and whispers   the drawls   the murmurs
the echoes   and on a clothesline I found on a beach
long abandoned by tourists   I hung and spread them
out   listened as the waves   so committed to ploughing
the shore   muffled the music your breath would often make
on nights when I could no longer feign the impression
of movement   how inch after measured inch
your lips   purpled   chapped   would scale new notes
between the shadows pulsing across my back
adding verses to my shoulders   refrains to my chest
experimental time signatures around my collar bone
and neck   And when they'd begin to receive too much
feedback from my skin   your tongue fatigued
with finding the right tone and pitch   I'd watch them
quiver to a heavy stop   each syllable unraveling
from the metaphor I had placed it in   That evening
the sunset lacked its usual confidence   The lines
continued to convulse   The waves made headway
weakened the sand from any sense of evenness
my feet sought   and as I lost sight of my ankles
the horizon melting upward   congealing the ocean
the jetties   the gulls   the scene   framed without obvious
reasons or context   shifted inland   where on a balcony
overlooking a courtyard   we stood in postures fit
for expatriates   and witnessed a herd of bulls
toss pedestrians   dressed like priests for mass
against the rails   windows   walls   And for every
bystander that was gored   for the limbs that flailed

for the blood that was splotched   you pulled
your hair behind your ears   bit your lower lip
and leaned farther out   wondering   it seemed
how the body could be so fragile   how it could just
lie there   as mournful as bouquets splayed
along a grieving sidewalk

## Postcard

For three nights   while you dreamt
of moonlit deserts   obese buzzards
carcasses consecrated with fresh bouquets
I joined the crowd in the town square
witnessed a gathering of widows tossing
their wedding dresses into a pile
One by one   they doused gasoline
and holy water   then danced   as they held
hands   around the growing bonfire
Applause and accordions rose around us
Stilt-walking jesters juggled bowling pins
frying pans   handed shirtless children
stickers and balloons   I moved in closer
hiked up my skirt   and when the crowd's
interest had shifted   and the women
shut their eyes   let the self-induced hypnosis
continue   I flung in my garter   and drifted
from the center of the city   unaware
that I'd wake up on the beach the next
morning   find myself amongst mounds
of washed-up lampshades and chandeliers

# Dear _____,

When I went down to the gates
I looked out afar   sequestered fields
along a dim skyline   The air begged
for a more practical existence   No doubt
the migrant silence felt the same   Still
the wind heaved   The sun   spellbound
with expired vows   silhouetted a row
of scarecrows staked on the horizon's
edge   From a patch of rhododendrons
a flock of black birds rose   praising
with every frenzied flap and trill
the privileged shadows that don't
let themselves be erased

**Dear** _____ ,

You touch the window   your face
at the foreground of a room composed
of papered walls   unlit lamps
a rocking chair beside a nightstand
where your travels' last coin rests
Tonight   at least   this familiar house
will not refuse your stay   and if
your shadow fulfills its obligation
to step outside   no breeze will sigh
your expired names   Just beyond
the garden's gates   a figure drifts
toward the vagrant darkness   and the heath
embraces the bruises of light
that still remain

# Dear _____,

At last   the city dissolves
And when the time comes
you take me by the hand
lead me through a valley
of rubble   skulls   In this weather
the wind makes a mushroom cloud
of your skirt   You tug it down
Dust devils dance   duel
dissipate into copihue petals
then settle faithfully at your feet
When the wolves begin to howl
the sun drapes your freckled skin
and the shadows cleansing
the powdered bones   leave no signs
on how to translate the distance
between our breaths

# Requiems

# Vigil

When the wound on my ribs
grew wide enough to fit your fingers in,
you pulled out flower petals: forget-me-nots,
orchids, rhododendrons you spread
on our bedsheets and pillows,
wondering why blood had yet
to compliment my skin. Dusk
and nightfall traded barbs across
the blinds, vied for a sense of closure,
and as the seasons changed—years
disguising themselves as seconds—
more petals spilled out: daises,
jasmines, geraniums, and those roses
that days later, when my eyes finally
closed, you placed on my eyelids,
hopeful they would grant me passage
to another world.

# Requiem

Late June, and the landscape—parched
and partly deserted—feels lethargic enough
to consider us protagonists. We watch,

from beneath the shade of an upturned
kiddie pool, the trailer park elders lumber
onto lawn chairs, jam their hands inside

their mouths, pry their dentures out, and dip
the rotted implants into buckets and spittoons,
as though attempting to deep-fry the false enamel,

saturate old inflections into a semblance
of speech they can finally chew. For hours,
they jaw at each other, switch between dialects

we doubt even they understand, and when dusk
scrawls a decent epilogue for their tales,
and their eyelids flutter between sleep and wakefulness,

we run from yard to yard stealing their dentures,
then smuggle them in our shirttails to the outskirts
of town, where we see the distant remnants of towers

struggling to remain important, and where a tree
stands with a horde of mannequins hanging
from its branches, naked and hoisted upside down.

There are holes drilled into their torsos,
there are cactus petals duct-taped to their lips,
and because you're certain that it was us

who had hung them there, that in our past lives
we scaled the bark and tied each up—hoping
they'd turn into wind chimes or piñatas—

I drop my share of teeth on the ground,
kneel before the bodies, and wait,
as the tree begins to shake, for these sins

to no longer claim me as their host.

# Sleep Start

[Hypnagogia]

Nightfall, and I'm at your wake again.
Your aunts sit shoeless on the couch,
debating new gossip, while men
in oversized suits stand in the foyer,
sipping coffee with old country rumors.
A piano stammers in the background.
A glass breaks in the kitchen. I approach
your coffin, and in your place lies
a mannequin in a wedding dress.
I lean in, embrace your plastic skin,
and as I attempt to cement fragments
of this scene, your face begins to melt,
begins to slip through my hands
as I cup what I can of your puttied flesh,
stuffing your nose, lips, and cheeks
inside my pockets, hopeful that when I leave,
your body, or what's left of it,
will remain unnoticed.

[Hypnopompia]

Morning, and you wake up
surrounded by mirrors, a trope
you find heavy-handed, but one
that you accept, pushing each
until a passageway opens, reveals
a dirt arena. The stands are filled
with cardboard cutouts of people,
and the music—as melodic as a windup
box—fades when the ringmaster
chants your name. You move
toward the center, where vultures
are chained to cannonballs,
where one-eyed men swallow swords
and machetes, and where a jester
kicks up dust, leaves in his wake
a lamb hoisted and bound, ready
for the choice you knew
you'd always make.

[Wakefulness]

That fall, I'd imagine your throat
as a small drawer, polished
and fit with a handle chiseled
from declarative statements,
and with enough room to hide
important fables, stories, to store
and inventory the novelty
of my voice, the whispered
hymns still caked to my lips,
the teeth and tongue that sometimes,
in their sudden carelessness,
were molded to all the wrong
questions, and that compelled me
to resort to the backside
of my fingertips, invent a soft dialect
along your jaw. And as I'd reach in
to remove the pauses, interjections,
the drawer would quickly close,
and my hands would stammer back
across my chest, unable to pronounce
this new language of doubt.

[Insomnia]

Nothing but the feeling of freefall
from here, apnea, debt and depravation,
a newfound state without the weight
of narrative, without the sense of feigning
oneself back into balance; no remedies,
folklore, no store-bought dreamcatchers
to wrangle in the moon from its daytime
insomnia, and still not enough self-will
to stimulate the slow and waning side-effects
of caffeine, to convert the mind
to the temporary doctrine of paralysis,
so when the body decides to settle
beyond siestas, to rejuvenate at the urgent
pace of a wound, I'll forget every petty
phrase about what absence does and does not
create, and let my cold sweats thaw
against you, till there's no sheeted distance
between us left.

# Requiem II

As punishment, you wake up
in a playground, naked, goose fleshed,
unsure why the slides, seesaws

and springers are warped, twisted,
shaped beyond any one synonym.
You rise, watch the sun bless

the city walls in the distance,
and once you've accepted
the barbed wire on the fences,

and the howls rising from the infant
darkness, you touch the swing sets,
remember how you'd become—

in the face of gravity's disapproval—
a hawk, a jet, a missile meant

to mutilate the ground, or to at least
pound it with your knees and hands,

so that it wasn't soil, grass, but a space
no longer graced with obligation,

purpose.

# Requiem III

Again, the sky molts its mood
to the middle of October,
and as the body bag of night

unfolds across the bruised
mountain ranges, the village children
approach you wearing goat heads.

They wobble side to side, adjust
to their new weight and vision,
and after locking arms, stomping

their feet in unison, they spin
like carousels, as you stare on,
dazed by the blurriness,

and blindsided by the knife
you begin wiping on your trousers;
the bloody fabric stained into

a Rorschach test. You decipher
butterflies, spiders, a bush anointed
by lightning, flames. And when

you gaze at your hand again,
you find a clump of bile dripping
from your palm. You hold it up,

examine its steady pulse,
the thump thump thump that echoes
somewhere in its center, provokes

the mass to bubble and you to place it
on the ground, watching, in the half-
darkness, as a set of fingers begins

to form, as the small hand that emerges
reaches out and touches your toes,
then suddenly retreats back into itself,

forcing you to drop to your knees,
to search the remnants for something,

anything you can keep.

# Exoduses

I

A sparrow—wrapped in rope
and barbed wire—lies inside a vase.
The vase sits on a table. The table
foregrounds a window framing
a desert, and in the center: a wake
of buzzards forms a halo in the sky.
We follow them, zoom in as their shadows
scythe a piñata lying on the ground—
the perfect host for the clumps of gnats
and maggots that spill from its bat-
battered holes, and the perfect shot
to cut away from as the scene refocuses
on the window, the table, the vase,
and on the sparrow that begins to spasm;
its wings expanding through the cord
and wire, its eyelids shuddering,
suffering to stay awake.

## II

You awake to a family not your own.
There's a father in a top hat, dapper
in a black suit and early Chaplin mustache,
midway through a glass of whiskey.
Your new sister spins in circles, chants the names
of constellations, while your mother, plopped
on a rocking chair, hums to the wounded crow
in her hands. You look at your father;
he looks out the window. A city rests beneath
shades of fog and snow. And though you prefer
to see a desert splayed across the window –
the ground playing host to every metaphor
carrion evoke—darkness still roams
the rooftops, and the endless rows of lights
pulse along the skyline—their symbolism
forcing you to consider that of the room's:
scabs of pink paint, graffitied portraits,
a floral-patterned border that tapers into
spider nests, mold, and which you ignore
when your father turns on his side, cranks
the recliner, expecting you to keep watch
over something that hasn't happened yet,
and that won't, at least not tonight,
not as snowfall whirls at the windowsill,
not when you choose to press your nose
on the cold, aching glass.

## III

June. And on cue, nightfall scrawls
its prologue across the horizon.
You enter the pier. Move past
the empty ticket booths, the rusted
turnstiles. And as you amble down
the strip—a string with a red balloon
tied to your wrist—you submit
to the park's emptiness. Still,
the Ferris wheel spins. Zoltar,
caged behind his glass, tells
a recycled fortune to the wind.
Lumps of cotton candy nuzzle
your feet, and though everything
is ownerless—the concession stands,
the games, the coasters—you walk
deeper in, until, minutes later,
you come upon a carousel, run
your hands along the horses.
For some, their heads are missing.
For others, the eyes and muzzles
are cracked, caved in. You think
of the symbolism. You think
of a childhood filled with broken
objects. You remember that red rocket
outside a supermarket, its flight path
so vertical, and yet so unexpected,
and because you've not yet forgotten
how quickly you were pulled from it—
two motherly hands redefining
gravity—you straddle a horse
and wait, as the music turns on,
to see what other moments, if any,
are worth recreating.

IV

And when the wind
stops kissing your neck,
you loosen your tie,
toss your suitcase in a bin.
The rails moan in the rusted
distance. You sit on the platform's
edge, contemplate the philosophy
of tracks, and wait till your body
becomes numb, succumbs
to gravity's vow.

V

Then, you wake up in a bathtub
ripe with algae, ash, with swarms
of dead mosquitoes, beetles, gnats.
You inhale, reach down, feel
the stale geography of your skin,
feel a pile of hair dryers whose cords—
hanging from the tub—are plugged
deep into the ground. You exhale,
stand up. The grime and gunk calcifies
into scales, and though you notice
the water below you rising—bubbles
frothing at your shins—you remain
inside, wary of what it means
when you take your first steps.

VI

We

swing

on meat hooks,

heretics

displayed

for the sinful

the sinless.

Recite a sermon

with me,
beg

for brevity,

forgiveness.

VII

The horizon shuffles its pages to December,
and I enter the plot in medias res, enter a field
filled with heaps of barbed wire, burnt lumber,
of ashes that scatter away from my feet.
The fog thickens to a new description. The pine trees
fade back into themselves, and though the scene
before me bares no evidence, I remember how
winters ago I burrowed my hands beneath the snow,
divided the whiteness from the whiteness,
until I found the body of a small goat: its neck
bent backwards, its horns sawed off, its mouth
halfway open, angled toward a pocketknife
I felt I once held before, and which now compels
me to reach over, grab the handle and point
the blade at my torso, unconcerned if I tighten
the grip, if the steel repeats a familiar prayer
between my ribs.

VIII

Nine months later, and as the morning lines
arrive like a godsend, you let the marble architecture
take you in, let the voices around you consecrate
your supple skin, while the opal, womb-shaped clock
in the center slices the minutes off the hour,
and the hours on each of its four faces—perhaps sensing
their importance—begin wandering like patrolmen:
slow, methodic, suspicious of everyone in the terminal,
and of how you reach inside your soaked, trench-coat
pockets, pull out a ticket with another name
written on it.

## Acknowledgments

The poems in this collection first appeared, sometimes in slightly different versions, in *The Carolina Quarterly*, *Juked*, *INCH*, *Neon*, *Yes Poetry*, and *Zone 3*. Thank you to the editors and staff at those journals.

Thank you to Sneha Subramanian Kanta, Issam Zineh, R. Joseph Rodríguez, and Daniel Lassell for their insight and input into earlier versions of this manuscript.

"Sleep Start" is dedicated to Stephanie. Thank you for always being a source of inspiration, partnah!

Thank you to Edward Vidaurre, jo reyes-boitel, and everyone at FlowerSong Press for their support and belief in this work.

And thank you reader.

# About the Author

Esteban Rodríguez is the author of six poetry collections, most recently *Ordinary Bodies* (word west press 2022), and the essay collection *Before the Earth Devours Us* (Split/Lip Press 2021). He is the interviews editor for the *EcoTheo Review*, senior book reviews Editor for *Tupelo Quarterly*, and associate poetry editor for *AGNI*. He currently lives in south Texas.

www.ingramcontent.com/pod-product-compliance
Lightning Source LLC
Chambersburg PA
CBHW011224120626
46545CB00010B/3147